BUSINES
THAT GE

BCS, THE CHARTERED INSTITUTE FOR IT

BCS, The Chartered Institute for IT, is committed to making IT good for society. We use the power of our network to bring about positive, tangible change. We champion the global IT profession and the interests of individuals, engaged in that profession, for the benefit of all.

Exchanging IT expertise and knowledge
The Institute fosters links between experts from industry, academia and business to promote new thinking, education and knowledge sharing.

Supporting practitioners
Through continuing professional development and a series of respected IT qualifications, the Institute seeks to promote professional practice tuned to the demands of business. It provides practical support and information services to its members and volunteer communities around the world.

Setting standards and frameworks
The Institute collaborates with government, industry and relevant bodies to establish good working practices, codes of conduct, skills frameworks and common standards. It also offers a range of consultancy services to employers to help them adopt best practice.

Become a member
Over 70,000 people including students, teachers, professionals and practitioners enjoy the benefits of BCS membership. These include access to an international community, invitations to roster of local and national events, career development tools and a quarterly thought-leadership magazine. Visit www.bcs.org/membership to find out more.

Further Information
BCS, The Chartered Institute for IT,
First Floor, Block D,
North Star House, North Star Avenue,
Swindon, SN2 1FA, United Kingdom.
T +44 (0) 1793 417 424
F +44 (0) 1793 417 444
(Monday to Friday, 09:00 to 17:00 UK time)
www.bcs.org/contact
http://shop.bcs.org/

BUSINESS CASES THAT GET RESULTS

Carrie Marshall

Published by BCS Learning & Development Ltd, a wholly owned subsidiary of BCS, The Chartered Institute for IT, First Floor, Block D, North Star House, North Star Avenue, Swindon, SN2 1FA, UK.
www.bcs.org

PDF ISBN: 978-1-78017-4563
ePUB ISBN: 978-1-78017-4570
Kindle ISBN: 978-1-78017-4587
Paperback ISBN: 978-1-78017-4556

British Cataloguing in Publication Data.
A CIP catalogue record for this book is available at the British Library.

Disclaimer:
The views expressed in this book are of the author and do not necessarily reflect the views of the Institute or BCS Learning & Development Ltd except where explicitly stated as such. Although every care has been taken by the author and BCS Learning & Development Ltd in the preparation of the publication, no warranty is given by the author or BCS Learning & Development Ltd as publisher as to the accuracy or completeness of the information contained within it and neither the author nor BCS Learning & Development Ltd shall be responsible or liable for any loss or damage whatsoever arising by virtue of such information or any instructions or advice contained within this publication or by any of the aforementioned.

Publisher's acknowledgements
Reviewers: Oliver Lindberg and Elizabeth Harrin
Publisher: Ian Borthwick
Commissioning Editor: Rebecca Youé
Production Manager: Florence Leroy
Project Manager: Sunrise Setting Ltd
Copy Editor: Mary Hobbins
Proofreader: Barbara Eastman
Indexer: Matthew Gale
Cover design: Alex Wright
Cover image: Denis.Production.com
Typeset by Lapiz Digital Services, Chennai, India.
Printed by Hobbs the Printers Ltd, Totton, Southampton, UK.

CONTENTS

Author   viii
Preface   ix

1.   **INTRODUCTION: WHAT IS A BUSINESS CASE?**   **1**
     Key takeaways   3

2.   **THE KEY QUESTIONS YOUR CASE NEEDS TO ANSWER**   **4**
     What is the need that your business case addresses?   4
     What evidence do you have to demonstrate the need?   5
     What are you proposing to do to meet the need?   6
     What are the other options?   7
     How does your business case fit with the appropriate mission, strategy and values?   8
     What disbenefits are there?   9
     How will you know you've achieved what you set out to do?   10
     How long will it take to implement?   11
     What are the known unknowns?   11
     What do you need?   13
     What will the impact on the business be?   13
     Key takeaways   14

3.   **THE IMPORTANCE OF IDENTIFYING EVERY STAKEHOLDER**   **15**
     Stakeholder identification   15
     Winning over stakeholders   18
     Key takeaways   20

4.	**HOW TO STRUCTURE YOUR BUSINESS CASE**	**21**
	How to present your business case for a large project	21
	Things to consider when you write your business case	25
	Key takeaways	26
5.	**BENEFITS AND OUTCOME ANALYSIS**	**27**
	What benefits mean in a business case	28
	Making soft benefits harder	28
	Money, money, money	29
	Analysing outcomes	29
	Key takeaways	30
6.	**THINKING ABOUT RISKS**	**31**
	Political risks	32
	Economic risks	32
	Social risks	32
	Technological risks	32
	Legal risks	33
	Environmental risks	33
	How to present risks in a business case	33
	Key takeaways	35
7.	**ROI: WHAT IT IS AND WHY YOU NEED TO SHOW IT**	**36**
	ROI basics	36
	Expect the unexpected	37
	Other financial measures	40
	Key takeaways	42
8.	**INTERNAL OPPOSITION: THE ENEMY IN THE RANKS**	**43**
	Fear of change	43
	Force of habit	44
	Lack of knowledge	44
	Key takeaways	45
9.	**MAKING YOUR CASE WITH A PRESENTATION**	**46**
	The rule of three	46
	Three is the magic number	47

Expect the unexpected   48
Key takeaways   49

10.   THE IMPORTANCE OF EDITING   50
Key questions to ask as you edit   50
How to make your business case better during
the editing process   51
Peer review   55
Key takeaways   55

11.   SUBMITTING YOUR BUSINESS CASE   56
Who should you submit your case to?   56
What should your business case include?   57
How should you format your business case?   57
When should you submit your business case?   58
Key takeaways   59

12.   AFTERWORD   60

References   62
Index   63

AUTHOR

Carrie Marshall is a journalist, copywriter, ghostwriter and broadcaster from Glasgow. A professional writer for 20 years, she has written thousands of features, columns, reviews and news stories for a huge range of magazines, newspapers, websites and trade publications. As a copywriter she has crafted copy for some of the biggest names in the technology, retail, audio and finance industries, and as a novelist she sold enough copies of her self-published debut to buy a car. Not a great car, but still: a car! Under various names, Carrie has written 11 non-fiction books, co-written six more and co-written a six-part Radio 2 documentary series. She blogs at bigmouthstrikesagain.com and tweets as @carrieinglasgow.

PREFACE

A business case is a very important document: whether it's printed out or delivered as a presentation, its job is to persuade an organisation to do something differently. That might require significant upheaval, significant investment or both, and that means even the brightest idea may face resistance.

Putting together a business case is rather like putting together a legal case, although it's a lot less likely to be made into a movie. You're putting forward an argument and providing evidence to back it up. If your argument is persuasive enough, you'll get the result you want: the green light to go ahead.

In this book we'll consider the techniques and tips that get results.

In Chapter 1 you'll discover what a business case is and how it's different from other documents, such as project proposals.

In Chapter 2 we'll determine the key questions that your business case must answer.

Chapter 3 is all about stakeholders, the people who will be affected directly or indirectly by your preferred course of action.

Chapter 4 looks at the mechanics of putting your business case together and what key sections it should include.

In Chapter 5 we'll identify the importance of identifying and quantifying the benefits your business case is designed to deliver.

Chapter 6 is where we become Eeyore, and consider what might possibly go wrong – and what we can do to prevent that from happening.

In Chapter 7 we get our spreadsheets out to calculate return on investment (ROI) in different scenarios.

In Chapter 8 we look at friendly fire, the internal opposition that can make implementing change more difficult and the strategies you can use to avoid and address it.

Chapter 9 is about presentations and how to utilise them effectively.

Chapter 10 discusses how to refine your business case to get the maximum effectiveness.

Chapter 11 highlights the steps to successfully submit your completed business case.

1 INTRODUCTION: WHAT IS A BUSINESS CASE?

No business is perfect, and no business will ever be perfect. There will always be a way to do things more efficiently, more cost-effectively, more environmentally responsibly – and in our ever-changing, high-tech world, what's impossible today will often be unremarkable tomorrow. And that means there will always be a need for somebody to put forward a business case.

A business case is a written argument, a proposal for making things better. It could be a simple idea expressed in a few paragraphs – 'if we switched to this supplier, we'd spend a lot less' – or it could be a thick document that's taken months to put together. But at heart, every business case says the same thing: something should be done, and here's how to do it.

No matter how complicated or detailed it may be, or how many appendices it has, every business case addresses five key questions: why, what, how, when and who.

The answer to the first question, the why, looks at the status quo and identifies the reasons why it isn't good enough. If everything was just fine, you wouldn't be proposing to do anything differently.

The answer to the second question, the what, details the changes you think are necessary to address the issues you've identified.

The answer to the third question, the how, explains the mechanics of what needs to be done – as well as how much it's going to cost and how long it's likely to take.

The when is all about timescales. Will this change be overnight, or will it need to be approached in stages? If there will be disruption or downtime, how long will that last?

Finally, the answer to the fifth question, the who, details the person or people who are going to actually make it all happen.

A well-researched, well-argued and well-written business case can make the difference between a project being rejected out of hand and a project being enthusiastically green-lit.

A business case isn't the same thing as a business proposal, although there's some overlap between the two kinds of documents. A business proposal is a much shorter, less detailed document. Your proposal essentially says: 'I have an idea!' Your business case is where you deliver the detail: why your idea's time has come, what benefits it will bring and what's needed to make it happen. Its job is to persuade a decision maker to approve the project and to agree to provide the necessary resources.

A business case is also different from a business plan. A business plan is a strategic document for the entire business; a business case is for a single strategy or project. Deciding to expand into China is a job for a business plan. Suggesting standardising field staff on iPad apps or moving to a hosted software solution is a job for a business case.

In this book we'll explore the key attributes of successful business cases. We'll dive into the key questions every business case must answer, the challenges of corporate inertia and internal opposition, the traps that can make a compelling case fail and the importance of identifying not just the people who'll be involved in your proposed changes, but the people who'll be affected by them too. We'll look at the big picture and the little details, from how to structure your business case to how to calculate return on investment (ROI) for different scenarios. And we'll discover how PowerPoint can be a force for good if you approach presentations in the right way.

KEY TAKEAWAYS

- A business case is longer than a proposal and covers different things. A proposal says: 'I have an idea!' A business case has the detail.

- A business case is for a single project or strategy. A business plan is for the entire organisation.

- A business case says 'Here is what needs to be done' and backs that up with evidence.

2 THE KEY QUESTIONS YOUR CASE NEEDS TO ANSWER

Every story answers questions. In books, those questions may be: Who is this person? What happened to them? How will they overcome it? In comedy they may be: What did the skeleton say to the barman? In music: How did it feel when everybody was kung-fu fighting? Your business case needs to do the same – and the first question you need to answer is: What do you want to do? In order to answer that, you'll need to detail not just the what, but the why.

WHAT IS THE NEED THAT YOUR BUSINESS CASE ADDRESSES?

'Lead with the need' is a very useful phrase in all kinds of business writing. It means stating the issue you're going to address, and it's really important to get that bit right. Leading with the need doesn't necessarily mean focusing on a problem that has to be solved, although of course that's often the reason for putting a business case together. The need could also be a plan to implement something that's of evident value to the organisation, such as doing something in a more resource-efficient way or taking advantage of a new technology. The need should be clear and convincing: when you express it, everybody should agree that yes, Something Must Be Done. If people don't buy into that bit, persuading them to do anything is going to be exceptionally difficult. It's also crucial to define the need as precisely as possible. What exactly will your business case deliver?

Douglas Adams' novel (1979), *The Hitchhiker's Guide to the Galaxy,* illustrates this in a typically astute and amusing way. In the story, a race of hyper-intelligent, pan-dimensional super-beings create Deep Thought, a computer that will calculate the answer to 'life, the universe and everything'. It costs unimaginable sums and takes seven and a half million years, but in the end, they get the answer to the ultimate question of life, the universe and everything:

'42'.

When the computer creators' descendants are outraged, Deep Thought confirms that the answer is the correct one: the answer to the ultimate question of life, the universe and everything really is 42. 'I think the problem, such as it was, was too broadly based', it explained. 'You never actually stated what the question was.' It is absolutely crucial that you don't try to give people your answer until everybody is clear what the question, or in this case, business need, is.

WHAT EVIDENCE DO YOU HAVE TO DEMONSTRATE THE NEED?

Presenting your case is rather like being the prosecutor in court: you can't just point at the defendant and say 'he did it!' even if he did indeed do it. You need to present evidence that proves he did it.

Business cases are just like criminal cases in that respect, although thankfully they're a lot shorter and nobody gets thrown in prison. The more evidence you have that things need to be done differently, the more receptive your audience will be. That means you aren't just the lawyer, but the detective too. You have to build the case by gathering enough evidence to demonstrate that the culprit was Professor Plum, in the library, with a lead pipe – or more likely an obsolete operating system, across ageing PCs, with unacceptable levels of downtime. Or whatever evidence is appropriate for the changes you're proposing the business makes.

This evidence isn't just necessary for the business case, it's important for the implementation of your proposal too. As I detail later in this chapter, we need to identify the things we'll monitor in order to check that our solution is doing what we want it to do. How do we know we have arrived if we don't know where we started from?

The evidence you provide will of course depend on the kind of need you're defining. For example, if you were proposing investment in a new telephony system, you might produce evidence of dropped or missed call rates or frequency of customer hang-ups – or, if you can't get that evidence, the very lack of evidence demonstrates that your existing system doesn't have the reporting tools you need. If you are advocating changing from a managed service provider, you might use service uptime statistics or outage statistics. Or you might be advocating hardware changes and use maintenance costs or helpdesk call volumes.

Wherever possible, the problem should be quantified. If you can also hang a pound or dollar sign on it, better still. 'We need to do this because it's costing us X/losing us Y/encouraging Z to buy from our rivals' is a very compelling point. The more money you're asking to spend, the more important such figures will be.

One useful question to ask yourself in this section is 'So what?', especially when it comes to less tangible benefits. For example, you might say that your solution delivers better customer service – so what? What effect will that have on the business?

WHAT ARE YOU PROPOSING TO DO TO MEET THE NEED?

This is where you set out what you propose to do. You've identified and quantified the 'why?', so now you can detail what precisely you think should be done. Start with the big picture and get into the detail: *this* is the best way to address *that*, because ... xyz.

WHAT ARE THE OTHER OPTIONS?

Sometimes there's only one possible option, which makes this bit easy, but most of the time there are several different ways in which you could address the business need, and each approach will have its pros and cons. In order to make your case, you need to demonstrate that you've taken every possible approach equally seriously, and that the option you're recommending is demonstrably the best one. That might require a full cost–benefit analysis of every option, or a detailed exploration and ranking of each option's risks and issues.

This section should also include the option of doing nothing. Let's look at that one in detail.

What if we don't change anything?

One of the biggest obstacles any business case faces is inertia, especially if the proposed changes will cost a lot of money or involve a lot of disruption. Then there's what *Harvard Business Review*'s Donald Sull called 'Active Inertia' (1999), which is when an organisation is too wedded to a particular way of doing things to even consider changing. Sull described the mental models that shape how managers see the world, calling them 'strategic frames':

> Strategic frames are the mental models – the mind-sets – that shape how managers see the world. The frames provide the answers to key strategic questions: What business are we in? How do we create value? Who are our competitors? Which customers are crucial, and which can we safely ignore?

> By focusing managers' attention repeatedly on certain things, frames can seduce them into believing that these are the only things that matter. In effect, frames can constrict peripheral vision, preventing people from noticing new options and opportunities.

Technology has given us countless examples of that. The traditional record industry did not embrace digital music until it had almost destroyed their entire business. Wikipedia made printed encyclopaedias obsolete. Smartphones and tablets, long mocked by PC firms as toys, dominate personal computing. Kodak was destroyed by the very digital cameras it helped to invent. And so on. These are all extreme examples, of course. But the cost of doing nothing isn't necessarily zero; choosing not to invest in something today could prove to be a very expensive mistake in the long term. If you can demonstrate – without exaggeration – the dangers of the status quo, it can really boost your case.

HOW DOES YOUR BUSINESS CASE FIT WITH THE APPROPRIATE MISSION, STRATEGY AND VALUES?

Does your business case help the business achieve its stated goals? Those goals might not necessarily or solely be financial or sales goals. For example, reducing energy usage also ties in nicely with many organisations' environmental corporate social responsibility policies. Or your proposal may assist with regulatory compliance or other key business issues.

This is particularly important in very large organisations, in the public sector and in the third sector, where organisations often have very detailed mission or value statements, strong regulatory frameworks or other criteria that must be adhered to. It's also important if your business case intends to take advantage of funding that has very specific criteria, or if it's relevant to government procurement. For example, the UK government has extensive policies in place that all of its suppliers must adhere to. The most recent versions of those policies are available online at www.gov.uk/guidance/public-sector-procurement-policy.

It's also worth thinking about the public relations (PR) value of what you're proposing. Can the changes you propose be used to market the company, portray it in a better light or otherwise make people feel warm and fuzzy about your organisation?

That's not going to be relevant if you're proposing a supplier swap, but it's worth thinking about with larger-scale projects.

SETTING A STRATEGY

Wherever possible, your business case should align with your organisation's strategic goals. Such goals might include:

- Create innovative new products or services.
- Deliver exceptional customer service.
- Identify new revenue streams.
- Boost growth in specific sectors or territories.
- Produce market-leading products or services.
- Reduce costs and/or wastage.
- Streamline core business processes.
- Ensure regulatory compliance.
- Enhance corporate social responsibility (CSR) goals such as community outreach, ethical supply chains or environmental footprint.

WHAT DISBENEFITS ARE THERE?

A disbenefit is the opposite of a benefit. Some projects will create disbenefits as well as benefits: for example, automation may make an organisation more efficient, but it might also reduce the number of people the organisation needs to employ in that department. Disbenefits can be external as well as internal: having a 24-hour distribution hub may be great for a retailer, but not so great for the people having to endure 24-hour trucking.

HOW WILL YOU KNOW YOU'VE ACHIEVED WHAT YOU SET OUT TO DO?

Once you've defined your need, you need to define how you'll measure success. For example, if your business case is about improving organisational efficiency, how will you know if it has delivered those improvements? If it's about boosting sales, what level of boost are you expecting? If it's about flexibility, how will you quantify that to be sure it's been worth doing? It's time to be SMART: setting specific, measurable, achievable, relevant and time-related criteria. A 10 per cent reduction in energy usage by April is SMART. A 10 per cent reduction in dropped calls over a three-month period, likewise. Not everything can be SMART. Many positives, such as improved morale, are hard to demonstrate on a spreadsheet, but you can still measure them indirectly. For example, a high staff turnover rate, sometimes called a churn rate, is often a sign of poor morale; if you can make morale better, that should have a measurable effect on the churn rate.

EXAMPLES OF SMART OBJECTIVES

- Use online meeting and collaboration apps to reduce business travel expenses by 10% in Q3.

- Train and support front-line staff in order to achieve average customer satisfaction rating of 4.5 stars by September.

- Improve ecommerce site cross-selling to boost average revenue per customer by 7% over the Black Friday sales period.

- Reduce average monthly dropped calls by 30% within six weeks of adopting new VOIP (voice over internet protocol) call system.

- Implement improved QA (quality assurance) processes to reduce product return rates by 5% within three months.

HOW LONG WILL IT TAKE TO IMPLEMENT?

Big changes don't happen overnight, and may require multiple stages. For example, a major IT investment isn't just about chucking a bunch of machines into a room and plugging them in. There are migration issues and training issues, support issues and logistical issues, and there may well be disruption or downtime; ensure these are factored in as much as possible to time estimates in your business case.

Timescales are important for several reasons. The first and most important reason is that investments rarely happen in isolation, and their implementation may impact other parts of the business: if resources are being used for your project, they may not be available to other parts of the organisation. Conversely, there may be other plans in the pipeline that could affect the viability, practicality and effectiveness of your project.

And of course, there's the money. If there is a significant financial cost to your project, then the organisation needs to be sure that its costs fit with existing or planned budgets.

WHAT ARE THE KNOWN UNKNOWNS?

What assumptions have you made, what issues have you taken into consideration and what potential problems could affect the outcome? If external organisations are involved, what happens if they don't deliver? Do your financial projections still make sense if costs or interest rates go up?

In other words, what's the worst that can possibly happen? It's acronym time: Project managers use RAID to remind them of the areas they should consider: it stands for risks, assumptions, issues and dependencies.

A **risk** is something that might happen, and which would have a negative impact. If the risk of it happening and the possible impact are significant, then you would detail the nature of the risk, its likely consequences and what steps you have taken or would be required to take to mitigate that risk.

That does not mean listing every conceivable risk, no matter how remote. Stick to the most realistic and significant risks.

An **assumption** is something that you believe to be true. For example, you might calculate the cost of a cloud-based solution on the basis of its current costs, and assume that those costs will either remain static or even fall in the future. Or you might calculate finance costs on the assumption that interest rates will continue to stay low. Such assumptions should be detailed.

While you're considering your assumptions, you should also consider any **constraints**. Constraints are things that limit your freedom and that are beyond your control. For example, there may be technical constraints such as having to use specific hardware and software that might not be exactly what you need. Or there may be legal or regulatory constraints, or simply resource constraints such as fixed budgets or the need to have a certain level of expertise from key contributors.

An **issue** is something that has already happened that you need to take into consideration. It's a risk that has already taken place, and in your business case you should outline what it is and what you're doing or propose to do about it.

A **dependency** is something that your plan depends upon, or that depends upon the success of your plan. List the key dependencies in your business case.

There are lots of very serious guides to RAID, but I prefer Steven Thomas' one in which he performs a RAID analysis for the likelihood of being smacked in the face:[1]

- Here, the **risk** is that somebody might smack you in the face.

---

1   See https://itsadeliverything.com/
risks-assumptions-issues-and-dependencies-dont-get-smacked-in-the-face

- An **assumption** is that it's safe to walk down a dark alley in the bad part of town without anybody smacking you in the face.

- An **issue** is when somebody has just smacked you in the face.

- And a **dependency** is when you need your partner to give you a lift so that you don't have to walk through a dark alley where somebody might smack you in the face.

It's a silly example, but it's much clearer than most of the management-speak that infests the more serious explanations.

WHAT DO YOU NEED?

In many cases, the answer to this one is money in the form of capital expenditure and operating expenditure. But it's not just money; it's people and time and training and any other resources necessary for the successful delivery of your business case. What are you asking the organisation to commit to?

Let's take an IT rollout as an example. In addition to specific hardware and software, you may need specialists of various stripes. First of all, you'll need to identify what skills you need; then you need to identify whether or not you have those skills already within your organisation. If you do have the necessary specialists in-house, you'll need to take them away from their other duties; if you don't have the in-house expertise, you'll need to hire specialists from outside the organisation.

WHAT WILL THE IMPACT ON THE BUSINESS BE?

Again, money is a factor here – you'll need to quantify what the exercise will cost (and, ideally, do so by taking best and worst-case scenarios into account). But projects involve more than just money. There's the use of physical resources and people's time, physical disruption and many other factors. If you're introducing new systems or changing existing ones, there's often a transitional period before any improvements are visible because people need time to get used to the new ways of doing things.

In most cases you'll be expected not just to identify what the impact will be, but also to identify how that impact will be managed. For example, you might schedule the implementation for after year-end or other busy periods, or you might require other projects to be paused, or request specific resources, such as the creation of a training hub.

KEY TAKEAWAYS

- Always lead with the need.
- Consider the bigger picture of organisational mission, strategy and values.
- Provide evidence that shows why your changes are necessary.
- 'Do nothing' should be one of the options you consider.

3 THE IMPORTANCE OF IDENTIFYING EVERY STAKEHOLDER

If you're a fan of business buzzword Bullshit Bingo,[2] you may flinch at the word 'stakeholder'; all too often it's used in a buzzword salad when 'customers' or 'staff' would do just fine. But it's a useful term when you're putting together a business case because it encourages you to look at the big picture.

A stakeholder is anybody who will be affected by an organisation, strategy or project. 'Affected' is the key word there, because you can be *affected* without being directly *involved*. I might not be involved in your hardware rollout, but if the new firewall stops me accessing something, then I'm a stakeholder. Your procedural changes might not affect my paperwork, but might lead to somebody demanding different data from me, and so on.

STAKEHOLDER IDENTIFICATION

If you don't know who your stakeholders are, then you haven't fully explored the potential impact of your proposal: the effect on stakeholders is a crucial part of any business case and you need to demonstrate that you've taken them into consideration.

So, how do you identify the stakeholders?

The best place to start is with the obvious stakeholders. That's everybody who will be directly involved in the changes you're proposing; so, for example, if it's a new app rollout, then your

---

2   See www.bullshitbingo.net/cards/bullshit/

stakeholders will include anybody who will be using that app. From there, you can zoom out to consider the people who may be indirectly affected. To stick with our app example, will there be a knock-on effect in helpdesk requests? Will training staff need to be involved? If the answer to either is yes, then those people are stakeholders too. For really big projects you might want to create a RACI matrix. It's not quite as sci-fi as it sounds, unfortunately; it's a spreadsheet with a big list of people and four categories: Responsible, Accountable, Consulted and Informed – hence RACI. Some people will be in one category, but some will fit into multiple RACI categories.[3]

A RACI matrix is sometimes known as a responsibility assignment matrix (RAM) or a linear responsibility chart (LRC), because goodness knows we don't have enough acronyms in business.

Let's discuss the categories more closely.

Responsible (aka recommender)

This is the person who actually performs the task. For example, if the task were training, then the person responsible would be a trainer.

Accountable (aka approver)

This is the person who signs off on the task and decides who'll do it: the trainer's manager, perhaps, or the financial controller.

Consulted (aka consultant)

The people whose opinions will be required on the task: people with expertise who won't necessarily be doing the work and with whom your communications will be two-way.

---

3 See www.cio.com/article/2395825/project-management/project-management-how-to-design-a-successful-raci-project-plan.html

4 Licenced under Creative Commons CC BY-SA 4.0. See https://commons.wikimedia.org/wiki/File:RACIQ_Chart_-_Responsibility_Assignment_Matrix.jpg

Figure 3.1 Example RACI matrix

Responsibility Assignment Matrix - RACI Chart

	Jeff	Michael	Reto	You	Alex	Anna	Bill	Cindy	Felix	Fred	Hans	John	Livio	Luc	Marco	Paul	Peter	Sue	Ted	Tim
Planning / Schedule	R	A	I	C					C											Q
Risk Management		I	I	Q						A								R		
Quality Management			R	C						R										A
Procurement				R		Q				R								R		A
1. Specifications Listing		C	A	R	Q			A		R								R		R
2. Site Requirements				Q	A						R									
3. Call for Tenders						R	C				R							R		
4. Budget Approval				A	Q					R							R			R
5. Contract Negotiations			A		Q	R	R											R		

* R – Responsible (works on), A – Accountable, C – Consulted, I – Informed, Q – Quality Reviewer

Image by Kockcharov, from Wikipedia[4]

Informed

These are the people who will be kept up to date with the project's progress, usually in the form of one-way communication to notify them of milestones met.

Let's take you as our example. You are responsible for creating your business case and accountable too, but you may consult with business analysts or other specialists. The board will expect to be informed.

This is overkill for smaller projects, but it's a very useful tool for complex projects and/or organisational structures. For smaller and/or simpler projects or organisations, a straightforward project organisation chart will be fine.

WINNING OVER STAKEHOLDERS

In many cases, the audience for your business case will be your manager or other executives, either inside your own organisation or in a client or potential client's organisation, and what they care about will be money: saving it, making more of it or wasting less of it. If you can make a persuasive case that doing X will either save or make money – even if it's in abstract terms such as improved morale, better customer satisfaction or better use of resources – then you're likely to receive a sympathetic response. However, money isn't the only consideration. In his famous book *How To Win Friends and Influence People*, Dale Carnegie (1936) writes:

> Personally, I am very fond of strawberries and cream but I have found that for some strange reason, fish prefer worms. So when I went fishing, I didn't think about what I wanted. I thought about what the fish wanted. I didn't bait the hook with strawberries and cream. Rather, I dangled a worm or grasshopper in front of the fish and said: 'Wouldn't you like to have that?' Why not use the same approach when fishing for people?

Everybody has the same question: 'what's in it for me?' But different stakeholders will require different answers. The financial director will have different priorities from those of the head of marketing; the HR department will have different concerns from the warehouse. That's important, because your business case needs to speak the language of the people you're speaking to. You need to identify the benefits that apply to the particular stakeholders you're addressing. Even in a relatively small group such as an executive board, your stakeholders may have different priorities and perspectives. What's in it for them?

Speak the right language

Audiences fall into four main categories, although of course there's some overlap between them. They are:

- experts;
- technicians;
- management;
- end users or customers.

When you're making a business case, you'll often find that you're asking the experts for information that you'll then use to help make your case to your audience, which will usually consist of people from the other three categories.

For example, if you're making the case for an IT hardware upgrade, you'll be explaining the technical issues to management in order to get the go-ahead; if you're making the case for a proposed change to existing ways of doing things, you may be communicating with technicians or end users.

Each of these audiences will expect different kinds of information. Experts don't want background information, because they know the subject inside out. End users don't want a barrage of tech data. Management often just want to know the bottom line.

In addition to our audience categories, there are also audience characteristics. One of the most important such characteristics is background knowledge. That might be practical knowledge, theoretical knowledge or a mixture of both. There's also education and background to consider too. Your goal is clarity, and that means using the right language for your readers. Language that's just fine for somebody with a degree in mechanical and electrical engineering and 20 years in high-tech fabrication may not be fine for someone whose expertise is in human resources. *EastEnders* references might not translate well for somebody in the company's Indian operation. Comparing something to the size of a London bus or to Wales only works if they can instinctively picture the size of a London bus or Wales.

One solution is to actually show a picture of a London bus, or of Wales. Not all information works best as text: it may work better as a visual, or as a table; it might be best expressed in a simple chart, or a more complex diagram. Different people have different communication preferences, and if you can tailor your case to the decision maker or relevant group's preferences, it really aids effective communication.

It's important to craft your business case for the people who will be reading it. That means focusing on what they need to know and delivering it in the most effective way possible, and using the right medium for your message.

KEY TAKEAWAYS

- It's important to craft the business case for the people who will be reading it.
- Stakeholders are not necessarily directly involved, but they may be indirectly affected.
- Different stakeholders may have different priorities.

4 HOW TO STRUCTURE YOUR BUSINESS CASE

A business case has four key jobs to do:

1. Explain the problem: lead with the need.
2. Describe the possible options, including doing nothing.
3. Recommend the best solution.
4. Explain how it will be implemented.

Throughout your business case, it's important to be as careful with words as you would be if you were writing an advertisement or brochure. Avoid waffle, jargon and wild guesses, keep your sentences simple and short, and don't present anybody with dense blocks of text. You might not be selling a product, but you're still selling something.

HOW TO PRESENT YOUR BUSINESS CASE FOR A LARGE PROJECT

One of the simplest ways to present a business case is a four-part structure:

- executive summary;
- project definition;
- finance;
- project organisation.

However, that structure can be expanded a little bit, like this:

- executive summary;
- statement of the problem or issue;
- full analysis of the current situation;
- list of possible solutions, including doing nothing;
- cost–benefit analysis of each possible solution;
- recommended solution;
- proposal for implementation.

It's the same thing, just presented in a slightly different way. We'll stick with the slightly simpler four-stage version, but the second one is just as valid and just as effective.

For really large or complex cases, you might want to break the categories down further.

The **executive summary** is the bird's eye view of the proposal and it's best to write it last when you have all the facts and figures at your disposal. It's a short summary of the entire business case, and it should tell the person or people reading it everything they need to know without going into detail.

The **project definition** is where you provide the background to your proposal: here's the issue, here's what I propose we do about it, here are the benefits it will bring and here are the risks, potential limitations and issues it will raise.

Identifying the benefits is part of the 'lead with the need' we explored in previous chapters. It is the 'why?' to your business case's 'what?': the increase in revenue, the reduction in wastage and the improvements that are not only possible but necessary.

As you'd expect, the **finance** section answers the million-dollar question: how much is this going to cost? Last, but not least, there's the **project organisation** section, which says who will be doing what and how progress and success will be monitored. This section will include SMART objectives and RACI analysis if appropriate.

Let's consider each section in turn.

Executive summary

If it's going to be a fairly detailed document, then it's a good idea to start with an executive summary. This is the business equivalent of the film industry's elevator pitch, where you sell a movie idea in a sentence or two – so, for example, *Alien* was '*Jaws* in space', and you could describe the *Twilight* movies as 'Jane Austen meets Dracula'.

An executive summary doesn't have to be quite that short – a written executive summary can be a few pages long if necessary; you can't always encapsulate complex ideas in a few sentences. However, it does need to focus on selling your idea, not crossing every T and dotting every I. That's what the rest of the document will do. Your executive summary is a sales pitch. You're telling a story, and if you can't sum it up simply, then you're going to find it difficult to enthuse others. It may be the first thing the reader sees in the document, but it's the last thing you should write.

Project definition

This is the section where you explain why the business needs are not currently being met, what the causes of that are and what needs to be done to address the issue. If there are multiple possible solutions, you detail them here and analyse each one to identify the pros and cons, and risks and benefits of each. That doesn't mean including every conceivable solution; just the most relevant ones. The goal here is to demonstrate that you haven't just chosen the first solution you encountered; you've come to recommend a particular option because you believe it fits most closely with the objectives of the organisation and provides the best benefit–cost ratio.

WHAT IS A BENEFIT–COST RATIO?

A benefit–cost ratio (BCR) is a rough guide to whether something offers value for money. I say rough because it's purely based on money – and like many calculations, its results depend on what you feed it. To borrow an old IT adage if you put garbage in, you get garbage out.

To calculate the BCR, you divide the total expected benefits of a project by the total expected cost of implementing it. If the benefits exceed the costs, then you have a positive benefit–cost ratio; if the costs exceed the benefits, you'll have a negative benefit–cost ratio. For example, if your BCR is 0.98 then for every pound you spend you're getting £0.98 back, which isn't very appealing; if it's 1.2, then for every pound you get a much more attractive £1.20.

In practice it's a little bit more complicated than that because you also need to factor in discounting – money will be worth less over time because of inflation and other costs.

Finance

This is where you break down details such as hardware costs, training costs, support costs, software licencing and any other quantifiable expenses. This section should generally include a contingency fund, because projects rarely run entirely to time or budget. This is where you'll detail the ROI calculations. More of that in Chapter 7.

There are two kind of expenditure here: operational expenditure (OpEx) and capital expenditure (CapEx), sometimes called PP&E for property, plant and equipment. CapEx is the money you spend on fixed assets such as buildings and servers. OpEx is the money you spend on keeping things running. For example, a laser printer is CapEx and its consumables are OpEx if you buy them outright; however, if you hire or lease the printer, it's an operating expense because you don't own it. Buying servers is CapEx; subscribing to a cloud-based service is OpEx.

If finances are not your area of expertise, it's really important that you involve somebody who has the relevant knowledge, such as your company's finance team or your manager. This section of your business case is crucial, and if the numbers don't add up or don't paint the right picture, your proposal is likely to be rejected.

Project organisation

In this section you detail your proposed implementation strategy: what needs to be done, when it needs to be done, who needs to do it, who's accountable for any issues and how you propose to monitor progress to ensure that everything is going according to plan. Monitoring will usually involve identifying and tracking hard information such as hours worked or money spent, but you can also standardise monitoring of softer outcomes such as customer satisfaction by creating a standard measurement tool, for example an online questionnaire. And some outcomes can be monitored indirectly; so, for example, improved customer satisfaction may lower a customer 'churn' rate or increase average revenue per user.

This section is where you list the SMART goals you identified previously, and might also include details of what reviewing would be done after the proposed changes have been implemented.

THINGS TO CONSIDER WHEN YOU WRITE YOUR BUSINESS CASE

A business case should be as short as possible without cutting corners. By all means show your workings by providing details of every single financial cost and projected benefit, but leave the granular detail to the appendices. That way the people who need that detail can get it, and the people who don't, don't have to wade through it.

Be wary of advice along the lines of 'Begin your executive summary with language such as "this report is submitted in support of X. Provided is an evaluation and analysis of all relevant financial, marketing and business costs/ considerations" ...', zzzzzzzzzzzzzzzz Sorry, I nodded off.

By 'be wary of' I mean 'pay no attention to'. A document that's as boring as that before you've even got to the end of the second sentence isn't going to win hearts or minds.

Business writing shouldn't be as informal as other forms of writing, such as this book. It should be precise and professional, but it needn't sap the reader's will to live. If you write plainly and economically, and make good use of graphs, tables and images, you'll achieve much more in a lot less time, with a lot less effort and over considerably fewer pages.

I'll make this statement many times in this book: your business case is a sales document. Its job is to persuade people that what you're proposing is a brilliant idea that should be funded completely and immediately. It may be a formal written argument rather than a few snappy slogans, but the objective is the same: to convince the reader to do something, in this case accept your proposed course of action.

KEY TAKEAWAYS

- Every case has four key jobs: explain the need, describe the options, recommend a solution and explain how it will be implemented.

- Write the executive summary last, when you have all the key facts and figures.

- Keep it short, but not too short.

5 BENEFITS AND OUTCOME ANALYSIS

A business case is a proposal to create a specific outcome: if we do this in this way, these are the benefits the business will receive. And that means identifying what the desired outcome actually is.

A business outcome is the result you expect from a specified course of action.

In many cases, the desired outcome is improved profitability from cost-cutting or organisational efficiencies, but there are other useful outcomes that may matter in specific industries or sectors. For example:

- Improving customer satisfaction can deliver increased sales via return business.

- Reducing customer churn can minimise customer acquisition costs.

- Widening a product portfolio can increase average revenue per user.

- Replacing ageing IT can reduce maintenance costs and avoid future financial headaches.

Successful business cases have clearly defined outcomes with clearly defined benefits to the organisation. But what do we actually mean by benefits?

WHAT BENEFITS MEAN IN A BUSINESS CASE

A benefit is something that delivers an advantage. That is often a financial advantage, such as reducing costs or maximising the bang you get for your bucks. Financial benefits typically fall into one of four categories:

- increasing income;
- reducing or avoiding outgoings;
- bringing forward income;
- postponing outgoings.

Such benefits are easy to express: if we do this, we'll increase profits by 10 per cent, or cut our premises management costs by 7.3 per cent; if we don't buy the latest server architecture this year, it's likely to be 7 per cent cheaper for us next year. However, other benefits are less tangible. For example:

- It might improve legal or regulatory compliance.
- It may lay the foundations for a bigger project, or help to avoid pain or expense in the future.
- It may deliver other 'soft' benefits.

A soft benefit is something that's hard to show on a spreadsheet, such as improved employee morale or customer loyalty. Wherever possible, it's a good idea to try and harden those benefits.

MAKING SOFT BENEFITS HARDER

The simplest way to harden a soft benefit is to put a price tag on it. You can't put a number on employee morale, but you can assign a value to days lost via absenteeism or the costs of recruiting new staff, which are often symptoms of poor morale. Similarly, you can't quantify better customer service, but you can quantify sales numbers: better customer service may well result in increased sales or higher average revenues per customer.

MONEY, MONEY, MONEY

Let's look at our financial benefits in more detail. What do we mean when we talk about 'income' and 'outgoings'? In most organisations, they mean cash flow, profit and loss. Cash flow and profit are ultimately the same thing, but the difference is timing: you can have a very profitable business, but encounter periods of negative cash flow during any month when more money is going out than is coming in. There's often a significant gap between doing the work (or making an investment) and getting paid (or the investment paying off).

This is one reason why it's crucial to include timescales in your business case. A proposal for a project that will make the business more profitable may have a very significant negative effect on the business's cash flow while the proposal is being implemented. That impact may require mitigation (borrowing, perhaps, or reorganising existing financial plans), or it may mean the project cannot be implemented in the form or at the time you're proposing.

ANALYSING OUTCOMES

Your business case will propose a course of action to achieve your desired outcome. To do that effectively, you'll usually need to carry out an outcome analysis. That needn't be formal, but it should include the following:

- The outcome: what result are you considering?
- What business objectives does the outcome support?
- Which stakeholders will be affected?
- What performance targets will need to be met?
- What risks may affect the outcome?
- What assumptions have you made?
- What will you need in order to achieve the outcome?
- How will you know that you've achieved it?

KEY TAKEAWAYS

- A benefit delivers some form of advantage to the business.
- Try to quantify intangible, 'soft' benefits.
- A business case can deliver profits, but also cause negative cash flow.

6 THINKING ABOUT RISKS

A risk is anything that can have a negative impact on the course of action you're proposing. For example, let's say you were proposing a series of seminars. What would happen if, as in December 2017 in the UK, unexpectedly heavy snowfall brought the country to a standstill and your delegates couldn't attend? Or, as in November 2017, a computer glitch grounded flights and your speakers couldn't appear?

There are strategic risks, where a course of action may interfere with the business's other objectives. That might be an opportunity cost – the money spent on your business case would not then be available to pay for X, Y or Z – or it might be that your case will have a knock-on effect in other parts of the business. For example, it may raise issues with regulatory compliance.

There are technical risks too. For example, if you're replacing an existing PABX (private automated branch exchange) telephone system with a brand new telephony system, will there be a period when parts of the business won't be able to talk to their customers? If you're upgrading servers and your business operates round the clock, will it be possible to perform the upgrade without any downtime?

There's an acronym for this: PESTLE, which stands for political, economic, social, technological, legal and environmental. In large or complex business case documents you may need to consider some or all of these types of risk. Let's look at each one in turn.

POLITICAL RISKS

These are risks relating to government policy. Brexit is a good example of such risks: if the UK does indeed leave the European Union in 2019, for example, many organisations will have to deal with changes to tariffs and to the movement of goods and people within the EU, changes to licencing (such as the licencing of medicines and the location of financial institutions' headquarters), trade deals and logistical issues such as the potential understaffing of and delays at border crossings.

ECONOMIC RISKS

These are the most common kinds of risk to consider: what happens if operating costs go up, suppliers hike their prices or interest rates rise? Could a financial shock make your proposed course of action bad for the business? We'll look at this in more detail in the next chapter.

SOCIAL RISKS

Social risks are about the outside world and are mainly relevant to international businesses. For example, if you're setting up new premises in a different country, there may be a different working culture in that country or demographic issues that might affect recruitment.

TECHNOLOGICAL RISKS

Technological risks could be disruptive technologies – Uber vs traditional taxi firms, Netflix vs traditional TV – or they could be organisational issues such as cybercrime or data security. There is also the issue of technology failure if your business case is based on using new technology in your organisation, and of competitors copying your technology if you're in the innovation business.

LEGAL RISKS

These are the risks of changes in legislation or other regulatory requirements. A good example of that is the EU General Data Protection Regulation (GDPR): its more stringent data protection regulation lost Facebook 1 million users in 2018.[5]

Legal risks also include safety. That doesn't necessarily mean risks to people from the physical implementation of your project. They could mean safety risks that may result from new procedures or technology. For example, you might not imagine that having someone run a social media account is particularly life-threatening. However, the London School of Economics and Political Science argues that social media falls under employers' duty of care responsibilities to ensure a safe working environment.[6] The well documented dark side of social media could be harmful for employees exposed to it.

ENVIRONMENTAL RISKS

This is about the physical environment, and includes the adverse weather I mentioned in the chapter introduction, the effects of climate change, the stability of energy supplies and the availability of resources. For example, smartphone and electric car production depends on supplies of rare metals that are very difficult to extract from the earth and which could face significant shortages as demand continues to soar.[7]

HOW TO PRESENT RISKS IN A BUSINESS CASE

Your business case shouldn't just detail the risks you've identified. It should analyse them and detail what you propose to do about them too.

---

5 See www.theinquirer.net/inquirer/news/3036570/
   facebook-loses-one-million-eu-users-to-gdpr

6 See https://blogs.lse.ac.uk/mediapolicyproject/2018/05/10/
   reducing-harm-in-social-media-through-a-duty-of-care/

7 See www.sciencedaily.com/releases/2017/03/170320110042.htm

In order to analyse risks, you need to do more than just say 'this might happen', no matter how true that may be. You need to identify the level of risk, and to do that you have to calculate the likelihood of it happening and the consequences of it happening. The higher the likelihood of something happening and the more damaging its potential consequences, the higher the risk level.

Risk levels are usually expressed as low, medium, high and very high, but you might find it easier to assign a number: for example, you might give a low risk rating the number one and a very high risk rating the number four.

Once you've identified the risk level, the next step is to prioritise them. The higher the risk level, the more of a priority it is.

Now for the hard bit. What do you propose to do about each risk? To answer that, you'll need to consider what is involved in dealing with the risk, in terms of both resources and people. How much will it cost, if the solution can be quantified in that way? How likely are you to succeed? What will you measure to know whether you've been successful or not?

There are four ways to deal with identified risks, or five if you're optimistic.

1. Accept it

This is the easiest option because it involves doing absolutely nothing. It's only appropriate for minor risks where the cost or disruption of dealing with them exceeds the trouble they are likely to cause.

2. Avoid it

Perhaps you've identified a risk of overloading the finance department. That risk may be higher around your company's financial year end, when finance staff are often exceptionally busy. If so, you could avoid that specific risk by rescheduling your plan for a quieter time of year.

3. Transfer it

This might not be possible if there aren't multiple parties involved in the project. It means getting one of the other parties to deal with the risk; so, for example, you might mandate that a contractor takes specific steps to address an identified risk, such as implementing a QA process to ensure code is error-free.

4. Mitigate it

We do this all the time in our everyday lives: we cannot stop it from raining, but we can mitigate its effects on our clothes by wearing a raincoat or carrying an umbrella. In business we might mitigate the risk of user error by providing extra training, or by enhancing an online help system, or by taking other steps to reduce the potential impact of an identified risk.

5. Embrace it

This one's for the optimists. Not every risk is necessarily bad. For example, having a product become such a big hit you can't make it quickly enough is the kind of risk you want to maximise, not minimise. In such cases you would plan for such a risk by identifying additional production capacity or outsourcing opportunities.

As with the rest of your business case, your risk analysis is about storytelling. In this case the story is: here's what might happen, here's how likely it is and here's what I propose we do about it.

KEY TAKEAWAYS

- Risks include financial changes, such as interest rate rises or cost increases.

- Consider technical issues, such as downtime or service availability.

- Safety does not necessarily involve hard hats.

7 ROI: WHAT IT IS AND WHY YOU NEED TO SHOW IT

Let's say you're an IT manager and you want the board to approve a significant IT investment. What is very important to you – the problems the investment will solve and the opportunities it will create – might not be very important to the board unless you can demonstrate the business benefits. More often than not, that means speaking the language of money – and in particular, return on investment, or ROI for short. If you can demonstrate an acceptable ROI, you're much more likely to get the investment you need.

ROI BASICS

ROI can be a very simple calculation. First of all, you estimate how much the proposed change will cost. Then you estimate the financial benefit it will bring. Deduct the cost from the benefit and you've got your ROI; so, if an investment of £8,000 would reduce operating costs by £10,000, you have an ROI of £2,000, or 25 per cent. The percentage is calculated against the cost of the investment, in this case £8,000.

Some benefits are easier to quantify than others. For example, your proposed investment might boost the morale of every user in the organisation, but that's hard to put on a spreadsheet. By all means, mention such benefits, but don't try and pin a financial value on them if you're just guessing.

You'll also need to pick a time period. ROI is calculated over a specified time period, usually the life of a project, because to begin with there are lots of costs and few benefits. By the end of the project that should be reversed: the money's been spent, and the benefits are everywhere. In IT, ROI is usually calculated over three to five years.

Whatever you do, don't rely on guesswork. Prediction is an art rather than a science, but if you're asking the board for money then you need to put forward a convincing case with realistic numbers. For example, your business case may be designed to reduce business travel by 10 per cent, or to reduce energy usage by 3 per cent, or to free up X hours per person. You'll need to show how you arrived at those figures too.

EXPECT THE UNEXPECTED

Investments don't happen in isolation. Changes in the outside world can make them more expensive or more risky, and your proposal may need to reflect that.

As I write this chapter, the Bank of England has approved the first base rate rise since 2007, raising the cost of borrowing. The cost of electricity has increased by 7.3 per cent since 2017, and while diesel is currently around £1.28 per litre, instability in the Middle East means that prices could soar to the same kind of levels we last saw in 2013, when a litre was £1.47. The pound is currently worth $1.31.

All of these changes have an effect. For example, the weak pound means many US IT companies are currently operating dollar-for-pound pricing, so a $999 iPhone costs £999 here in the UK and US-based services that charge in dollars per user per month are more expensive than they were just a few months ago. Components and consumables priced in dollars are more expensive for UK firms than they used to be. Increasing energy prices and fuel prices increases businesses' operating costs.

You don't need to consider these things if you're only asking for a couple of new PCs, but you do if you're proposing a significant long-term investment, because they can affect your ROI. An increase in borrowing costs and operating costs could make your project more expensive to implement, or the benefits less significant. As a result, for large project proposals it's important to state any underlying assumptions, such as assuming energy prices increase at the same rate or that wage levels won't increase significantly.

For large scale projects, a tool called the Project Discount Rate is used. It's a kind of reverse interest rate that tells you how much a sum of money you have today will be worth in the future. Let's say you have £1,000 in your hand today. The interest rate on savings accounts is effectively zero, but the cost of living goes up every year, so the spending power goes down. If the difference is 5 per cent, then £1,000 in today's money will only be worth £950 this time next year. If you've been too optimistic and the difference is 10 per cent, then it will only be worth £900.

When you include a percentage in your cash flow calculations, you are using the Project Discount Rate. If you're confident that your predictive abilities are much better than Mystic Meg's and that the risks to your project are very small, you'd use a very low rate. If there's a lot of supposition and risk taking, you'd use a high rate. Let's look at a real example. You're making the case for an IT investment that will cost £10,000, and you expect to generate positive cash flow of an extra £2,500 per year for five years. That's a £2,500 overall benefit, or 25 per cent – in theory at least. The next step is to use the Project Discount Rate to see what your real ROI is likely to be. The rule of thumb is that the closer to double figures the Project Discount Rate becomes, the more likely the project will deliver a disappointing or even negative ROI.

We'll consider two scenarios here. First, we'll be confident in our predictive powers and go for a low rate of 5 per cent, and then we'll look at the same proposal but with a lot less confidence and a Project Discount Rate of 10 per cent. To use the Project Discount Rate, you simply apply it to the cash flow prediction for each year – so to take 5 per cent off, you divide it by 1.05. After a year, £2,500 in today's money will be £2,381; in year two, it'll be £2,267; in year three, it'll be £2,159; in year four, it'll be £2,056; and in year five, it'll be £1,958.

Table 1 ROI using 5 per cent Project Discount Rate

	Year 1	Year 2	Year 3	Year 4	Year 5	TOTAL
Expected return	2,500.00	2,500.00	2,500.00	2,500.00	2,500.00	**12,500.00**
Actual value at year start	2,500.00	2,380.95	2,267.57	2,159.59	2,056.76	n/a
Project discount rate/year	5%	5%	5%	5%	5%	n/a
Actual value at year end	2,380.95	2,267.57	2,159.59	2,056.76	1,958.82	**10,823.69**

In total, then, our £10,000 investment will bring in £10,823. That isn't quite the 25 per cent return we had hoped for, but at just under 8 per cent, it might be enough to convince the board to go ahead.

What happens when we're less confident in the future? With a rate of 10 per cent instead of 5 per cent, the figures are: £2,272; £2,066; £1,878; £1,707; and £1,552. The total is therefore £9,476, which is a loss of just over 5 per cent. The board might still think the investment is worth it, but it will be a much tougher sell.

Clearly, we're looking at worst-case scenarios here, but that is an important part of making your case. If you don't consider the worst-case scenario, the board surely will.

OTHER FINANCIAL MEASURES

Your business may expect you to look at other financial criteria in the business case, such as net present value, too.

Net present value

Net present value (NPV) is used in budgeting to take account of the fact that money loses some value over time. For example, in 1987 your pounds went much further than they do today: petrol was 30p a litre and a pint of lager was 93p.[8]

That's an extreme example, but if you're given the choice of receiving £10,000 now or receiving £10,000 in 10 years' time, you should take the money and run. If you had chosen the first option a decade ago, that £10,000 would be worth £12,958 today.[9]

In budgeting, money received in the early stages of a project is worth more than money received later because of inflation and

---

[8] See www.liverpoolecho.co.uk/news/liverpool-news/youll-shocked-how-little-cigarettes-12922111

[9] Based on average inflation of 2.63 per cent from 2008 to 2018.

Table 2 ROI using 10 per cent Project Discount Rate

	Year 1	Year 2	Year 3	Year 4	Year 5	TOTAL
Expected return	2,500.00	2,500.00	2,500.00	2,500.00	2,500.00	12,500.00
Actual value at year start	2,500.00	2,272.73	2,066.12	1,878.29	1,707.53	n/a
Project discount rate/year	10%	10%	10%	10%	10%	10%
Actual value at year end	2,272.73	2,066.12	1,878.29	1,707.53	1,552.30	9,476.97

other pressures. That's not a concern with short-term projects, but if you're proposing something whose benefits will come in over a fairly long period, then you'll need to apply discounting to take account of the falling value of money. That's where the NPV comes in.

With NPV you choose a discount rate that reflects the declining value and apply it to your project. For example, if you choose a 10 per cent discount rate, then £10,000 in year zero becomes £9,000 in year one, £8,100 in year two, and so on. This is important when you're justifying significant expenditure, because money you spend now is spent at today's rate, not what it will be years from now – but any income will be based on what money is worth at the time, not today.

Let's take an example. If you want to spend £50,000 now and claim it'll pay for itself after five years, NPV says otherwise: assuming no income for the first year while you're actually implementing it, over five years it'll bring in £9,000 + £8,100 + £7,290 + £6,561 + £5,905. That's £36,856 not £50,000.

KEY TAKEAWAYS

- Decision makers may prioritise ROI over other factors, even if those factors make your life easier.
- When making financial predictions, don't just present the most favourable scenario.
- If you don't consider the worst-case scenario, the board surely will.

8   INTERNAL OPPOSITION: THE ENEMY IN THE RANKS

When you put forward a business case, you're essentially saying 'Let's do things differently.' And when you do that, some people will think 'why?', or 'let's not'. This is called internal opposition, and it's something you'll need to think about when you're putting your case together.

Internal opposition usually comes in three flavours: fear of change, force of habit and lack of knowledge. Let's examine each one in turn.

FEAR OF CHANGE

We are straightforward souls, we humans: we like our habits, our routines and our certainties. When someone comes along and suggests doing things differently, we often fear the worst. And to be fair, we've often got good reasons to fear the worst. Who among us hasn't experienced some bone-headed change, a change whose downsides were obvious to everybody in the company apart from senior management?

In order to address fear of change, we need to identify the specific fears people may have about our business case. People may fear disruption, or extra workload. They may fear that the change could make things less efficient, or make their day more difficult. It's much better to anticipate and allay such fears from the get-go than try and respond to them once you're facing pushback from internal opposition.

There's another variation, too: *Not Invented Here Syndrome*. It's a slightly sarcastic label for a real phenomenon that often occurs when a business case suggests bringing in a solution from outside the organisation or department. That solution may be a software package or a cloud service; it may be third-party expertise or just a method used by another bit of your business. Webopedia excellently describes it as having 'intensities ranging from a mild reluctance to accept new ideas all the way up to a raging software xenophobia'.[10]

Not Invented Here Syndrome can be connected to people's pride in their work, which helps to explain why some people are so resistant to change: they've spent a lot of time and effort learning and doing things in a particular way. Where appropriate, you may find that the solution is to collaborate rather than dictate; to ask people how your proposal can improve what they already do rather than replace it. As with other fears, this is best considered before you put your business case together.

FORCE OF HABIT

This is slightly different from fear of change or *Not Invented Here Syndrome*. It's not a conscious resistance to change, it's simply force of habit: people have spent years doing X, and may stick with it rather than start doing Y. Once again, this can be considered and allowed for in your business case so that you can identify any training and support that may be required both initially and once your proposal has been fully implemented.

LACK OF KNOWLEDGE

Many IT projects fail not because they're bad projects or use bad solutions, but because of ineffective communication. All too often people don't understand the reasons for change or

---

10 See www.webopedia.com/TERM/N/not_invented_here_syndrome.html

aren't given the necessary training and support they need to adapt to it. It's absolutely crucial that you think about how your proposed changes will be communicated to *anybody* who might be affected by them – and that means giving serious consideration to the people who will be affected by them.

KEY TAKEAWAYS

- It's better to anticipate concerns and address them head-on.
- Don't forget about ongoing training and support needs.
- Many projects fail because of ineffective communication.

9 MAKING YOUR CASE WITH A PRESENTATION

In some organisations, the decision makers may prefer you to make your case in the form of a presentation, with printed documentation provided for in-depth study; or you might just prefer to deliver it that way.

Like your executive summary, a presentation is best written when the rest of your business case is complete: it's the Greatest Hits version of your document. PowerPoint presentations[11] have developed a bad reputation over the years, but they can be very effective if used wisely and they're often very useful when it comes to making a case. They lend themselves particularly well to visual data such as charts and graphs: if you have sheaves of Excel printouts, they're best presented in the accompanying notes, not on the screen.

Less is more: your slides should accompany what you're saying, but they shouldn't simply detail everything you're saying. If they do, faster readers will speed-read them and ignore you altogether. Don't overwhelm your readers with detail. A single chart with an exciting figure and short caption will have more impact than 10 lines of cramped text.

THE RULE OF THREE

The first trick to successful presentations is to follow the rule of three, first set out by Aristotle[12] and used very effectively in all kinds of marketing materials and technology keynotes:

---

11 Other presentation tools are available, of course, such as Prezi and Keynote.

12 In his *Poetics*.

1. Tell them what you're going to tell them.
2. Tell them.
3. Tell them what you've told them.

For a great example of this in action, head to YouTube and check out any of Steve Jobs' keynote speeches from his second spell at Apple – the period when he introduced iPods, iPads and iPhones. The structure and repetition is even more obvious in the post-Jobs Apple, but as those executives don't have Jobs' legendary showmanship, they don't do it quite so well.

Step 1 is your very brief introduction: 'Today I'm going to demonstrate that X will make everybody's life better.' Step 2 is where you make your case; and step 3 is a brief recap of your key point or points: 'As we've discovered, X would make everybody's life better. Is there anything you'd like to ask me?' Step 2 follows exactly the same structure as making a case in writing. Once again, we tell a story. First of all, we lead with the need – here's an issue that needs to be addressed – and then we set out the available options, including doing nothing. From there we explain why our recommended course of action is the best option, and we then describe how that course of action would be implemented. Good presentations tell a story, and like any story the trick is to tell it well. That means editing, editing and editing a bit more. Could that bit be clearer? Would that bit work better as an image or a chart? Would those details be better left to the printed handouts?

THREE IS THE MAGIC NUMBER

There's another rule of three in presentations, which is to stick to three main points. That's because our brains like to remember three things at once, and it's why three-point phrases are so common in advertising, speeches and the arts. For example:

'Stop, Look and Listen.' (Road safety advert)

'Our priorities are education, education, education.' (Tony Blair speech)

'A Mars a day helps you work, rest and play.' (Advertising slogan for Mars bars)

'Friends, Romans, Countrymen, lend me your ears.' (Shakespeare's *Julius Caesar*)

'Truth, justice and the American way.' (What Superman fights for, DC Comics)

Many successful presentations have three sections, share three ideas and have no more than three bullet points on screen at once. It's a trick that also works in many other kinds of business writing too.

EXPECT THE UNEXPECTED

Don't forget about questions.

You can expect two kinds of questions. The first kind are the ones where you know the answer is a few slides away; the other kind are the ones asking for more information about the presentation you've just delivered. You can't script those, but you can prepare for them. In fact, you already have: your entire business case is about anticipating other people's questions and providing the answers. What will this cost? Who's going to manage it? What impact will it have? Why can't we do X instead?

You might find it helpful to create quick reminders so that you don't have to rack your brains or wade through a hefty document for the details. For example, if you think you'll need to talk in more detail about the financial projections, it might be helpful to have all the figures ready. I am a terrible pessimist, so I prefer to write or print my notes on little cards rather than keep them on a computer or tablet.

KEY TAKEAWAYS

- Tell them what you will tell them, tell them, tell them what you've told them.
- Three is the magic number.
- Be prepared for questions.

10 THE IMPORTANCE OF EDITING

Presenting a business case is like a moon shot: you only get one go at it. That means it's essential to ensure that the document you hand out or the presentation you deliver is as good as it possibly can be. And the way to do that is by editing it. If you have someone you can trust to cast their eye over your document, they're worth their weight in gold, but you can be a perfectly good editor yourself.

KEY QUESTIONS TO ASK AS YOU EDIT

Editing is the process of revising material before it's published or distributed. There are two parts to it. The first is asking whether the information presented is correct, and the second is asking whether it's being presented in the best possible way.

If you're taking part in a formal submission process, there's a third part: ensuring that you deliver exactly what you've been asked to deliver in the way you've been asked to deliver it. If the guidelines say the text should be in a Word document with double-spaced 12pt Times New Roman, it won't be accepted if it's a PDF with 10pt Helvetica. In business cases it's the first one that matters most: while professionalism is important, I don't know of any proposals that have been rejected because of typing mistakes or poor word choices. However, a business case whose sums don't add up is doomed from the outset. Ask yourself the following:

- Are the figures accurate?
- Are the figures verifiable?
- Are the figures consistent?

- If you've made assumptions, are they reasonable and documented?
- Is there anything you haven't included?
- Are any projections overly optimistic?
- Are any costs overly conservative?
- Are the numbers presented correctly?

That last one doesn't just mean watching out for typos, calculation errors or common mistakes such as getting percentages wrong. It means ensuring that the correct units are used, that any comparisons made are reasonable ones and, if charts are being used to demonstrate something or illustrate a point, it means ensuring that they don't use visual tricks that may mislead.

We've probably all seen the graphs on certain news channels whose improper scaling wrongly implies that the gap between two closely matched things is enormous, or that a chasm between two figures is hardly worth thinking about. Wikipedia has an entire section on the most common ways graphs can mislead:[13] please use it as an example of what not to do!

This is about credibility. If there's anything in your business case that suggests your numbers cannot be trusted, it can undermine the entire proposal. The next step is to print out your document and read it on paper. There's something about paper that means mistakes are much more obvious than they are on a screen.

HOW TO MAKE YOUR BUSINESS CASE BETTER DURING THE EDITING PROCESS

I've explored the mechanics of effective business writing in detail already and in the other books in this series,[14] but here is my own executive summary: less is more.

---

13 See https://en.wikipedia.org/wiki/Misleading_graph

14 *Business Writing for Technical People, Technical Writing for Business People, Writing for Social Media,* all published by BCS (2018).

- If you're using a lot of jargon, you can probably improve your document by using less of it.

- If your document is very wordy, you can probably improve it by using more precise language.

- If your document is packed with background information, you can probably improve it by concentrating only on the most relevant and important information.

- If your document has multiple authors, you can probably improve its tone and consistency by having no more than one or two people writing it.

Here are some common traps that are all too easy to fall into.

Too much information

The novelist Ken Follett is legendary for his research, not least because he can't resist putting all of it on the page: the three books of his famous Century Trilogy weigh in at a whopping 3,100 exhaustively researched and fact-checked pages.[15]

Don't be like Ken Follett in this way. That's not to say don't do your homework, but only put it on the page if it's absolutely necessary, because what works in literature really doesn't work when you're trying to sell something. Too much information makes any document hard going, and if the information isn't relevant, it may encourage readers to skip the bits that are.

The passive voice

A lot of business and public sector writing uses the passive voice, which can make even the most exciting idea sound utterly tedious. An example of the passive voice is when you say 'it was decided that' instead of 'we decided', or 'it has come to our attention that employees have been using their work PCs for personal web browsing' instead of 'don't use work PCs for web browsing'.

---

[15] See www.amazon.com/Century-Trilogy-Trade-Paperback-Boxed/dp/1101991550

As I was writing this chapter, a banking startup on Twitter, called @monzo, posted what looked to me like the perfect guide to the passive voice.[16] It made me laugh, but more importantly it explains the passive voice better than any grammar textbook ever could.

If you can add 'by monkeys' to the end of a phrase and it still makes (grammatical) sense, it's passive. For example:

- A decision has been made to close your account ... by monkeys.
- This bug will be fixed in the next update ... by monkeys.
- Your complaint will be escalated to second level support ... by monkeys.

You can't do the same with active writing: 'We've decided to close your account by monkeys' doesn't work, and nor does 'We'll fix this bug in the next update by monkeys.' The passive voice is the wet Wednesday of business writing: it makes writing much less interesting and therefore much less effective. It's best avoided, especially when you're trying to win people over.

Long sentences and endless paragraphs

It's much easier to read and process something short and to the point than sigh your way through endless, huge, dense blocks of text. Brevity works. In moderation. Not too much. That gets irritating. Like here. But it's a good idea to try and say as much as possible with as few words as you can. Mixing up short and long sentences works particularly well in longer documents.

When you're writing, take a look at it in full page view. Is it a forbidding rectangular block of words with precious little white space and sentences that go on forever, adding lots of words to

---

16 It's part of the firm's tone of voice guide, which is available on its website at https://monzo.com/tone-of-voice/

the original point without actually doing anything constructive, resulting in something that if you were to read out in one breath would have you keeling over because it takes so long to read that you'd run out of oxygen long before you reached the second-last comma, which came before another bunch of words that did absolutely nothing of any use whatsoever?

If you can't make the words work harder (you probably can), you can at least think of your readers and format your words in a less boring way. Break your paragraphs into shorter ones, use more white space and consider using a chart or diagram if it can do the job more effectively than words can.

Unhelpful big words and unfamiliar acronyms

Good writing is about communicating clearly. Using 'discombobulated' when you could say 'confused' or using an acronym your readers won't recognise isn't helping anybody.

Too many words

As the excellent guidebook *The Elements of Style* by William Strunk and E.B. White (1999) puts it:

> A sentence should contain no unnecessary words, a paragraph no unnecessary sentences, for the same reason that a drawing should have no unnecessary lines and a machine no unnecessary parts.

Clichés

Clichés have no place in a business case because most business clichés are meaningless. Your business case document needs to be rooted in reality, not throwing things at the wall to see what sticks, thinking outside the box or running things up flagpoles to see who salutes.

Woolly writing

'Woolly' is another way of saying vague, confused or lacking in clarity. When writing is woolly it's often because the person who wrote it didn't go through the simple steps of effective business writing: knowing what story you want to tell, knowing what you want your readers to do, and knowing where and how to address the people you want to communicate with. One way to avoid woolly writing is to plan what you're going to write in the form of bulleted or numbered lists. That's what I've done throughout this book: I decided what chapters I'd have, and then what topics I was going to cover in each chapter. Creating the skeleton first and fleshing it out later keeps us focused and on-topic, and that prevents duplication.

PEER REVIEW

If possible, get someone else to look over your business case before you submit it. They needn't be a professional proofreader, because sometimes all you need is a different pair of eyes to notice errors in the text, glitches in a document or things that just don't make sense. Everybody makes mistakes, but we're not always great at spotting them in our own work.

KEY TAKEAWAYS

- Editing improves almost every piece of writing.
- Your business case must be rooted in reality.
- Peer review can be useful too.

11 SUBMITTING YOUR BUSINESS CASE

The final part of the process is to actually submit your business case. How you do that depends on the organisation and on the kind of case you're submitting: some organisations are informal and don't have a submission process as such, while others – especially external bodies and public sector organisations – have very detailed submission policies. It's important to ensure you don't fall at the final hurdle by falling foul of such policies.

Let's look at a real example in this chapter, from Mersey Care NHS Trust.[17]

WHO SHOULD YOU SUBMIT YOUR CASE TO?

Every business case should have a known recipient, often known as a sponsor: that is the person or group of people who will evaluate your case and make a decision on whether to proceed. Formal submission guidelines will make this explicit, such as with our NHS example, whose guidelines state:

> You should first seek approval from the Clinical Business Unit Director, or Director or Head of Service before submitting the business case to the Capital Investment Group. The business case should state in writing that this approval has been obtained and that you have involved your finance lead in any proposed costings.

---

17 See www.eprescribingtoolkit.com/wp-content/uploads/2013/11/Business-Case-Guidance.pdf

Get that wrong and your case won't be considered.

Knowing who to send your business case to isn't just crucial to make sure it gets to the right person or place, it's also crucial because it tells you how you should pitch your business case in terms of tone and content. A case that must be submitted to the chief financial officer of an organisation will be very different from one that's to be submitted to the chief marketing officer.

WHAT SHOULD YOUR BUSINESS CASE INCLUDE?

I've given advice on structure elsewhere in this book, but always go with the organisation's guidelines if they have them. The NHS Trust provides extensive guidance on the sections they expect to be included in business cases and on details such as sources for financial information. For example, it asks for a full risk analysis and references between the proposal and the Trust's strategic objectives.

This kind of guidance is very valuable and it's crucial that you follow it:

> Every business case must be in line with at least one of the Trust's four key strategic objectives and not in conflict with the other three.

Public sector organisations are usually very good at providing detailed submission guidance. For example, here is the guidance from the Engineering and Physical Research Council: https://epsrc.ukri.org/research/facilities/equipment/process/apply/

HOW SHOULD YOU FORMAT YOUR BUSINESS CASE?

If the submission guidelines request specific formatting, you must use it. Otherwise go with the house style for the organisation, or stick to the business basics of clean, consistent typography and a clean, consistent layout.

For electronic submissions, many organisations will either ask for specific file formats (Microsoft Word is a favourite) or will ask you to complete online forms. In the latter case, make sure that your chosen web browser and plugins display the form correctly: for example, I often encounter forms that have clearly been tested on Windows PCs and which don't display properly on Apple's Safari.

WHEN SHOULD YOU SUBMIT YOUR BUSINESS CASE?

If there is a formal submission deadline, you must meet it: submissions received after a deadline expires will not be considered. It's a good idea to submit in advance of any stated deadlines just in case of any gremlins, and if you're submitting a physical copy by post rather than an electronic one, then it's wise to use a tracked, signed-for delivery service to prove that your submission was sent in time. Likewise, keep electronic receipts or screenshot the acceptance screens for online submissions.

When there's a formal deadline, there's usually an indication of when you should expect a response and/or a decision. If not, there's no harm in asking when you might expect to receive feedback on your case.

If there isn't a formal deadline, it's your decision when to submit your business case. If the organisational need your case addresses is urgent and important, then clearly the sooner you submit it the sooner you can save the day, but it's worth considering the wider environment: for example, if your business has seasonal peaks, it may be wise to wait for a slightly less frantic period to ensure that your case gets the attention it deserves. Similarly, if your case would require extensive resources that are already allocated for a considerable period, speedy submission may not be the best policy.

KEY TAKEAWAYS

- If there are formal submission guidelines, please follow them. Public sector organisations often provide very detailed guidance.

- Make sure you're submitting to the right person, especially in larger or complex organisations.

- If formatting isn't specified, stick to clean and simple formatting and standard file formats.

- Deadlines aren't optional.

12 AFTERWORD

In Chapter 2, I compared you presenting a business case to a lawyer presenting a case in court. That means the bit when you deliver your presentation or hand over your document is the equivalent of sending the jury away to deliberate over their verdict. You have presented your case, and all you can do now is wait for the decision.

There are some things you cannot control. Sometimes the necessary resources aren't available, or the changes you're proposing may conflict with other business activities; and sometimes even the most obviously beneficial proposals are not accepted. But the better your case, the more likely you are to get the verdict that you're hoping for.

As you've discovered in this book, the secrets to business cases that get results are actually very simple. A business case must provide a compelling argument that Something Must Be Done, and that argument must be backed with strong evidence and reliable figures. It must be tailored for the people who are going to read or see it, and to their particular priorities and requirements. It must align with the business's or organisation's objectives. It should be credible, and should take account of risks both internal and external. And it should be the right length: not so long that it bores everybody to tears, but not so short that it misses crucial detail either.

Some of the chapters in this book talk about writing style, and that's important: poorly written business cases can be hard work, and the more interesting and well-presented your business case, the more receptive readers will be. But although the way you tell your story is important, the story itself is what matters. If you remember to always lead with the need, to define the specific issue your business case is going to address, then your business case will largely write itself. All you need to do is polish it to make it even better.

Here's to many green lights.

REFERENCES

Adams, Douglas (1979) *The Hitchhiker's Guide to the Galaxy*. London: Pan Books.

Carnegie, Dale (1936) *How To Win Friends and Influence People*. New York: Simon and Schuster.

Strunk, William Jr and White, E. B. (1999) *The Elements of Style*. Harlow: Pearson.

Sull, Donald (1999) 'Why good companies go bad'. *Harvard Business Review,* July–August issue. Available from https://hbr.org/1999/07/why-good-companies-go-bad [26 November 2018].

INDEX

accepting risks 34

Accountable (RACI matrix) 16, 17

acronyms, unfamiliar 54

'Active Inertia' 7

Adams, Douglas 4–5

Apple 47

Aristotle 46

assumptions 12, 13

audience types/ characteristics 19–20

avoiding risks 34

Bank of England 37

BCR (benefit–cost ratio) 23–4

benefit analysis 27, 28–9

brevity 23, 25–6, 52, 53–4

Brexit 32

business plans 2

business proposals 2

buzzwords 15

calculations 50–1

CapEx (capital expenditure) 13, 24–5

Carnegie, Dale 18

cash flow 29, 38

churn rate 10, 25, 27

clichés 54

constraints 12

Consulted (RACI matrix) 16, 17

cost–benefit analysis 7, 22

cross-selling 10

CSR (corporate social responsibility) 8, 9

customer satisfaction 10, 27

deadlines 58

defining business cases 1–2

dependencies 12, 13

disbenefits 9

doing nothing 7–8, 21, 22, 47

dollar-for-pound pricing 37

economic risks 31, 32

editing 47, 50–5

embracing risks 35

end users or customers (audience type) 19

endless paragraphs 53–4

energy prices 37, 38

environmental risks 31, 33

European Union 32

Excel 46

executive summary 21, 22, 23, 26, 46

experts (audience type) 19

Facebook 33

fear of change 43–4

file formats 58

finance 21, 22, 24–5

financial benefits 28, 29, 36

Follett, Ken 52

force of habit 44

formal submissions guidelines 50, 56, 57, 58

formatting business cases 57–8

GDPR (General Data Protection Regulation) 33

goals/missions, organisational 8–9

graphs/charts 18, 20, 26, 46, 47, 51, 54

hard benefits 28
Harvard Business Review 7
How To Win Friends and Influence People 18

impacts 13–14, 15
implementation strategy 25
inertia 7
Informed (RACI matrix) 17, 18
interest rates 11, 12, 32, 37, 38
internal opposition 43–5
issues (RAID analysis) 12, 13

jargon 21, 52
Jobs, Steve 47

known unknowns 11–13
Kodak 8

lack of knowledge 44–5
language/grammar 19–20, 21, 26, 50, 52–5
large projects 21–5
legal risks 31, 33
licencing 32
London School of Economics and Political Science 33
long sentences 53–4
LRC (linear responsibility chart) 16

maintenance costs 6, 27
management (audience type) 19
measuring success 10
mental models 7
Mersey Care NHS Trust 56, 57
mitigating risks 12, 35
monzo 53
morale 10, 18, 28, 36

needs
    addressing 4–5, 7–8, 23
    demonstrating/evidencing 5–7, 8
    leading with 4, 21, 22, 47, 61
    your own 13
Netflix 32
Not Invented Here Syndrome 44
NPV (net present value) 40, 42

online collaboration apps 10
operating costs 32, 36, 37–8
OpEx (operational expenditure) 13, 24–5
opportunity costs 31
outcome analysis 27, 29

PABX telephone system 31
passive voice 52–3
peer review 55
PESTLE risks 31–3
political risks 31, 32
PowerPoint 2, 46

PR (public relations) 8
presentations 2, 46–9, 50, 60
procurement policies 8
project definition 21, 22, 23–4
Project Discount Rate 38–40, 41
project organisation 21, 22–3, 25
proofreading 55

QA (quality assurance) processes 10
questions (in presentations) 48

RACI analysis 16–18, 23
RAID analysis 11–13
RAM matrix 16, 17
recipients 56–7
regulatory compliance 8, 9, 12, 28, 31
Responsible (RACI matrix) 16, 17
risks 7, 11–12, 31–5
ROI (return on investment) 2, 24, 36–42
rule of three 46–8

slogans 26, 48
SMART objectives 10, 23, 25
social media 33
social risks 31, 32
soft benefits 28
stakeholders 15–20
strategic frames 7
strategic goals 9
strategic risks 31
strategy, setting 9

structuring business cases 21–6

Strunk, William 54

submitting business cases 56–9

Sull, Donald 7

technicians (audience type) 19

technological risks 31, 32

The Elements of Style 54

The Hitchhiker's Guide to the Galaxy 4–5

Thomas, Steven 12–13

timescales 11, 29

too much information 52

transferring risks 35

travel expenses 10

Uber 32

value statements 8

VOIP (voice over internet protocol) call system 10

Webopedia 44

White, E. B. 54

Wikipedia 8, 51

woolly writing 54–5

worst-case scenarios 13, 40